Where I began and Where I belong...

Journeys.

My Life and Spirit

TYE

SECOND EDITION

Book and Cover Design by Tyona Y. Ezeilo

ISBN 978-1-964776-06-4 (Hardcover format)
ISBN 978-1-964776-02-6 (Paperback format)
ISBN 978-1-964776-03-3 (eBook format)

Publisher:
Envisionry Media

Envisionry Media
Creativity & Inspiration

Please send book inquiries to Connect@Tyona-ME.com

*To Nana, Mary Catherine Shellow &
Grandma, Rozena McGee
I wish I knew your stories.*

Table of Contents

Table of Contents

Poems Continued	Page

Preface

Preface ~ The Window

Of all the content in this book, the next few pages have been the most difficult to release.

Where to begin?

Journeys© is a collection of thoughts and poetry that spans two decades of my life. In my journey from a twelve-year-old girl to a thirty-year-old woman, I enjoyed many blessings and learned many lessons.

I fell in love with the written word at a very early age. I still find myself mesmerized by the gift that is bestowed upon me when the stanzas within a poem (or lyrics wrapped in the melody of a song) move me to experience places and feel emotions too powerful to verbalize. Since I was a little girl, I have used the art of writing to release those things I could not otherwise share. Writing has been a welcomed shift from the spoken *(& unspoken)* word.

At the age of 13, I began writing Journeys©. My first bona fide poem, Beloved, was dedicated to my mother. I was born to her at 17 and my father, 18, in the winter of 1975. They each grew up in large, single parent families in Brooklyn's East New York. My mother was the middle child of nine and my dad, the third youngest of six boys. I never knew my grandfathers, but my grandmothers had each left their own parents' homes in the south as teens and moved to Brooklyn, New York during the Great Black Migration of the 1940s and 1950s.

When I was three, my parents married six months before my mother gave birth to my sister and only sibling. By the time I was 20, my parents' high school educations, devotion to one another and commitment to improving our living conditions had taken us from a 2-bedroom apartment in Crown Heights, Brooklyn to a 4-bedroom single family house in Palm Beach County, Florida.

My early memories of my father are of an athletic, studious, quietly driven man. He was on a city baseball league, read profusely, studied Islam and was more often the one my mother instructed to assist me with my homework. As a young girl, I was bothered by my mother's loudly repetitive insistence that my father help her cook, take care of the house, and watch my sister and me. She requested he spend less time

alone watching sports on TV and more time focusing on her and our family. From time to time, my mother would share with me her struggles with my father. She encouraged me to be selective when dating and to put my own dreams above any man's.

At the time, it would be impossible for me to see our family life through my mother's eyes. It was my mother who disciplined us harshly and my father who attempted to rein her in. Throughout my adolescence, I sometimes viewed my mother as the villain and my father and I as the persecuted. My mother's frustration with her living situation manifested in her profane rants for change.

My mom appeared to be my dad's complete opposite; outgoing and boisterous. For her, our family seemed to be both a source of stress, and the center of her world. She was fiercely protective and careful whom she trusted with our care. Her daughters were her treasures. She dressed us with matching outfits and hairstyles. Our hair was always neatly maintained, our clothes thoroughly pressed and our faces clean (and glistening). Our shared bedroom was fancifully decorated with special attention to our favorite colors and interests. She filled our rooms with books and baby dolls. She purchased two of every toy the other wanted. Hand-sewn curtains and linen laced our windows and covered our beds. She was the first to volunteer to assist in our classrooms, and she knew every one of our friends by name. She taught us to cook, braid, crochet, sew, type, clean, decorate ...and live.

As teens, my sister and I shared many of the same clothes, interests and friends. Although the time came when our friends and interests became hugely divergent, and her slender figure and my expanding girth made it impossible to share clothing, she would always be my dearest, and most vocal confidant.

In my childhood, most of which I spent in New Jersey, I had an ever-changing circle of close friendship ties. Bonds I am still unraveling today. Stories I may later share, once I discover how they want to be told. Pieces of one bond float throughout these pages. From the time I was 11, until I was about 20, there was one who occupied precious spaces in my life. I walked in his shadow. He was my first thought many mornings and my warmest worry most days. He was a good friend, a spirited brother-figure, and my first infatuation. My mother adored him. My friends desired him. All of which, in hindsight, made every moment he spent with me feel priceless. Our time together, however, was not without cost. Then, I did not recognize – appreciate – value- the price I was paying. He was undeniably the inspiration for my early writings.

Throughout junior high and high school, I was wrapped up in searching for what I thought my parents had – a forever partner – and I soon found one.

During my freshman year of college, two weeks before my 19th birthday, my 1st son's creative spirit was born into the world. His biological father and I had been a couple for almost 4 years (and would remain together for 2 additional years following my son's birth).

Let me take a step back.   My son's 1st father…

When I looked upon my 1st reciprocated love, I saw a beautiful person, inside and out. I was enchanted by his playfulness, his compassion for his friends, his love of my family, his rich mahogany skin, his thick dark eyebrows, and soft brown eyes. I was in love with him and believed we would be together forever. He professed to adore me and throughout our relationship (*and for years after*) he sent me love letters, "thinking of you" cards, and he kept all my secrets. He offered me his love and held me as if he were afraid to let go.

In some ways, we hurt each other deeply. In other ways, we expressed our unending love for one another deeply. Our love was young, our hearts were open. Meaning, we felt *everything* deeply. We said *everything* freely. And often, we did *whatever* we wanted. 'Love' was this undefinable "thing" we innately experienced. It was this **powerfully** magnetic "thing" we naively constructed and had little understanding of how to operate. Despite us both having relationships outside of ours, we were obsessed with whatever *IT* was we had begun to build together, and it kept us zealously holding on. Perhaps, all *young* love is that conflicted.

We experienced what felt like many lifetimes, together. And we continued to hold on. - For *so* long.

It did not seem as easy for him to embrace his role as father to our son. It's so painful to look back and remember our moment because my son has never truly known him. I look at their lack of a relationship and can only imagine what may have been. I finally accepted his physical absence in my own life, but it will always be heartbreaking to know all that he has missed and continues to miss with my (our) son. That was then. I am uncertain of how to speak of him, now. I have not been able to define the place for him in my present, nor my future. But I have also finally accepted that he is there, here, …somewhere. And will be for the rest of my lifetime.

The month I turned 20, my parents, sister, son, and I relocated to South Florida. That year, a year before I ended my relationship with my son's biological father, I would meet someone who would change my life. Someone with whom I would begin to fall in love. My future husband would be the first person other than my mother to encourage the development of this book. From our first meeting, his interest in me was bewildering. I believed I was too young and immature for him: *An unmarried mother with a year-old child, complex relationship, high school education, working a retail cashier position and who had mainly attended church for weddings.* He was five years older, dressed conservatively, an assistant store manager, recent college graduate and weekly churchgoer. I grew to care for him over profoundly heartfelt conversations and late nights talking about life. He showed interest in my perspective. I chased after him not believing we would ever be a couple but loving the attention he showed me.

In the early part of our relationship, I looked at him and saw pieces of everyone I had ever loved plus traits I had never anticipated I would desire. As our time together grew, I began to recognize the greatness of the differences between us, and it became a challenge to share our worlds. He described a fairytale childhood with pious parents and saintly siblings. Growing up with constant drama and multi-dimensional familial relationships, his life and family all seemed so alien to me. Soon I began to feel as though the only flaw in his otherwise comfortable existence was me. Later, I would discover extensions to his tales, gaps in his recollection. We struggled with commitment, my prior relationships, my place in his family, co-parenting and being true to our individual selves, together. We got married four years and one day after our first date. It took me years after meeting him to reprogram my thinking. To come to know that we are all flawed. To understand him: The things he shared with me and things he did not. It took years to stop believing in my inferiority, his superiority and still be able to love him. Those years changed me forever. Women who meet my husband for the first-time may rave about aspects of his physical appearance. They see an almond skinned, 6'5", marvelously sculpted man with a husky voice, luminous green eyes, and a dimpled grin – and though he **is** delightful to look at – what reveals his true beauty is his humor, his intellect, his kindness, his passion for life and his dedication to his family. My husband supported me emotionally through undergraduate studies and financially through graduate school. He cooks regularly, cleans regularly and is a loving, devoted, involved, and attentive father who has grown to tremendously appreciate my love. With my husband, I have been able to experience so much joy and live so many dreams. Our years as partners have also changed him. For our changes, willing compromises, I will always be grateful to God.

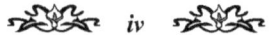

I am also thankful for the many miracles that followed our marriage. In 2001, I developed pre-eclampsia during pregnancy and in early fall as the world witnessed America being attacked, I labored in a hospital bed giving birth two months prematurely to a (thankfully) strong, healthy 3-pound baby boy. In 2002, I returned to school earning a bachelor's degree in social work from Florida Atlantic University. Then, immediately entered its graduate school to complete an advanced standing graduate degree program. After an 11-month hiatus to complete a work practicum in local schools and counseling centers, in 2003 I earned a master's degree in social work and returned to full-time employment working with families of children with developmental delays. In 2004, two days after Hurricane Frances hit south Florida (and thirty minutes after our arrival at the hospital) I gave birth to another amazingly healthy baby boy. Being blessed with the responsibility of raising three sons after realizing the significant role that men have played in my life, has been a humbling experience that led to yet another. In 2008, my youngest child was born, and I became a mother to an incredible daughter.

Compiling my potpourri of writings and diary entries into Journeys© has been an ongoing process that has met with varying degrees of complications.

Reflecting on my life and decision making has been both terrifying and enlightening. As a young woman, I sometimes found myself entangled in language. Even today, pushing to verbally extend myself socially as well as professionally and uncovering things I would have normally hidden has been awkward. I've spent decades of my life driven by my emotions but understood by my behavior, which was often a vast paradox. I now find that I too often reach for language to express what I know will never fully be understood. Releasing pieces of me to others for review has been such a frightening process. I am not a skilled writer or historian, and I am to this day uncertain of where I fit in.

So, why go through the effort of having these words bound and published and placed in your hands?

The gift of conversion.

In Journeys©, I have given you a glimpse into my life. Yet, I am still unsure whether my completion of this book is meant to serve as a window into my soul. But, in your hands its meaning and purpose is infinite, and maybe, for some, it will be a window into your own.

Tyona

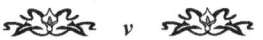

JOURNEYS
- The Beginning

Journey.

What a beautiful name of mystical intent.

The Journeys I take inside,
Inside my head,
Lead me to a world of Perfect Understanding.

The view from behind
the tunnels of my eyes,
Is too tempting not to follow.

I walk alone
and though my arms
reach out into the darkness
They are not met.

Yet, I sense a presence
So strong
So overwhelmingly tender,
That it cloaks me
and holds me
Suspended.

I cease in my journey.
Turning to seek out
my companion.

Such a foolish Explorer of the Unknown;
Discoverer of wasted time, broken hearts
& E n d l e s s Doubts.

A powerful cool breeze, 360 degrees,
Turns me.
It directs me,
and sets me at a faithful pace on my so desired path.

I stand.

Fingertips frozen solid.
Hands outstretched.
Eyes sealed;
For They Can No Longer Be Trusted to Lead Me.

Slowly, my inner lids begin to reveal
A jagged image
and the reflection off a shard piece of glass
Initiates THE CYCLE.

Beginnings

Beloved
- Mommy

Beloved is he,
        my darling child,
So Gifted ... as he may be.
        Yet all the while
Sad is my child
For things I cannot see.

Well-groomed is he,
        my darling child,
So hidden behind pretend glee.
        Yet all the while
Sad is my child
At things beyond my reach.

Confused is he,
        my darling child,
"There are secrets that I *must* keep."
        Yet all the while
Hateful is my child
Towards things that make me, me.

In Our Time

In our time
And down our line.

I battled yours
You battled mine.

We searched so hard
But could not find ...

Our freedom

I looked to you
You looked to me

Mirrored Images
We could be

Storming & Forming
Circles of Insecurity ...

Our Family

they linger

her family didn't talk much
or, at least that's what it seemed.
her family spoke not of profit.
they did not speak, much, of their dreams.

her family lived in secrecy.
feelings they didn't compare.
screams were often muffled.
inquiries,   no one would dare.

Yearning to know what others knew.
Yearning to prove her heartache true.
joining the others' painted smiles,
soon she'd learn, the pain could be filed -

away in her mind
hidden from view
laughing aloud
her insides bruised.

they looked at each other
but never revealed
the deadness their feeling
the bond that they shared.

though they all seemed to dwell
in their own earthly hell,
her family didn't talk much...

but, if they did...

oh, what stories they could tell.

Two May Know a Secret... Who will tell the truth?

*Darkness holds the secret why
She gave of herself so freely.*

*Darkness holds the key to why
She seemed to give in completely.*

*Images, dismissed as dreams
Suppression, which brought about relief.*

*Things which she should not have seen
play back on a mental movie screen.*

*Stories told of the undead
who live and grow within her head.*

*Secrets, held so sheepishly
of things that were deemed: unspeakly.*

*A young girl who did not understand
the desires and demands of a man*

*Often is talked of in hushed tones
(never spoken in her vicinity)
Even by those who know the truth to why:
Mere men affect her life so deeply.*

*Secrets, those which should not be told,
make rest embedded in our souls.
But when the parasites are unearthed within our roots....
Those who know our secrets
may not always speak our truths.*

My Everything

My father couldn't give
any more than he did.

My father couldn't show
with a hug or a glow.

That I made him proud.

My father couldn't say
that he loved me every day.

He couldn't conversate
or show interest in what I'd say.

My father couldn't see
Everything he'd be to me.

Still, my father taught me love
of books, of men, of all that was ...

Our past.

My father taught me pride
in the blood behind his eyes.

My father made me see
ALL that a husband should be.

He showed they should provide
for me a better life.

But they never had to be
head-over-heels in love with me.

Sometimes they might stray
but, never far away.

And as long as they remained
it would all be O.K.

My father has taught me much;
Even things he didn't want.

He has never apologized
for the tears behind my eyes.

Of course, he's sacrificed a lot
to give the family what it wants.

Therefore, there's no need to say
that he's ever made mistakes.

He has given me, all, I'll ever need.
After all, one man can not be everything.

Maturation

She was in love at 11
Spoiled at 12
Heartbroken at 13
A run away at 14
Suicidal at 15
Beaten at 16
Pregnant at 17
Undone by 18
Rescued at 19
Reborn at 20
And secured at 21.
Those who see her now comment,
"She's so mature."
Not realizing life for her ... has just begun.

Lovelorn
Lovelorn

Hide and Seek

There are few places to hide
        when you know you won't
               be sought.
"Never hide
        or lose your pride,"
that's what Momma always taught.
    I am proud to be a woman,
     as you are proud to be a man.
"Always try to seek out the wrong
and change
        whatever you can."
"But Momma, it's hard to reach the top
when you know you won't be seen."

   - Yet without at least trying -
       Is it worth it?

   Not to me.

Prizes

To relieve the pain
I try to gain
From whom shall I take the blood?

The next victim
   of he?
  Shall I listen to pleas,
So similar to my own cries?

I am sterile.
So young.
  He's the victor.
They've won.
  Yet the game never really began.

Who understands?
  No one gains, but
The petty and insane!
Who can collect prizes
  ... when everyone's ran?

Take My Hand

Take my hand
and lead me
  to the world
          beyond your eyes.
Lies - They have no meaning
          where
Truth and Love reside.
        There always is that place
        that too few of us explore.
Attempt to truly see me
and you'll find
        there **is** more.
                  See
You'll never lose
the battle.
We'll always win
                    the race.
        If we hold on to each other
        we'll always reach that place.

Forever:

Forever my heart
Forever my guide
Forever my strength
Forever my pride.

My lover
My soldier
My brother
My Friend

My Beautiful Black Diamond,
Forever My Prince

Please Tell Me

What can I give to you
that you will not throw back at me?
What can I say to you
that has not already been said?
What can I do for you
to make you love me?
Who should I be for you
tonight in bed?

Reflecting Expressions

If he
Smiled, a solitary smile,
    it would never be alone.
Puzzled over a difficult situation,
    his would not be the only mind occupied.
Eyes blinded by the deceitful,
    there were always others to protect him.

There are questions
        that need not be answered.
Feelings
        that need not be said.
The little things
        a lover reveals
The other lover
        has read.

In an empty room
If he reached out
        right then
there would always be a
        Reflecting Expression
reaching out to him
        again
                and
                    again.

De' Man(d)s

There is something to be said
About a man
with endless dreams.

A man whose countless missions
prevent him from accomplishing
a single thing.

There is something to be said
About a man
whose thoughts are deep.

A man who opens up to few
but has let you
take a peek.

There is something to be said
about the excitement
in his eyes,
the passion in his voice,
the hope that never dies.

A man who never bores you.
A man from whom
you'd buy a bridge.

A man who when beside you
...well, it's like...
gliding naked - off a cliff.

There is something to be said
About a man
who enters your head and body
with such force
altering your mind
rearranging your thoughts.

There is something to be said
About a man
who makes you laugh.

A man
that makes you glad
you take back
the things you said

and you
invite him
into your bed

despite

... the things

... he did.

Eyes

They have told me they want me.
They have told me lies.
They have doubted my faith
And even once cried.

They have warned me of danger
But were never surprised.
And have stammered through bolts of fire
When they've been high.

Yet, they have never said they loved me
Or even once tried,
To give me a glimpse of our future
As they enjoyed the ride.

Ere the Baseline:
Forever, Your Groupie

She looks at him
A man
      Bold
       and
         Proud
of Black and Brown.
Standing tall
Knowing all
  He leaves nothing to be
       desired.
(He's in disguise)
     but
in her eyes
he could never be a
liar.
     Taking women in his home
     Leaving no place else to roam
He intimidates them with his
wit
Never learning when to
quit
     One quick lie and then it's done
     Another life has now begun
With smooth unsoothing lips of
       reverence
Worsening things with utter
        ignorance
Now her bed is neatly made
All the cards set and laid;
    She needs his help.

She looks not once
but
many times again

And hoping
To at least find

A Friend.

She looks at him

A man.

Then realizes
that all
the while

He's been looking back…

Just a child.

Precious
Precious
Wildflowers
Wildflowers

T I M I N G

If alone
I'd find happiness
with the blood of you
within my own self.
Yet it's not the day
      it's not the way.

Younger
Too younger
than yourself myself
I wonder
Will we reach that day
      not far away.

Younger
Too younger
than myself right now
I wonder
Will we want to reach that day
      too far away?

To My Baby

In My Prayers ...

I pray that your eyes are not blinded by love,
          and that your heart is not closed to it.
I pray that you use your fists to knock down walls,
          and your hands to build bridges.
I pray that you give comfort to those who are
          sick and lonely and tired.

I pray that your mind thirsts for knowledge,
          hungers for solutions,
and learns to appreciate the differences of this world.

I pray that your strengths overshadow your weaknesses,
          that you are honest and faithful,
                    loved and respected,
                         and that you become a guardian,
          and never a victim of anything or anyone.

I pray that you develop a strong sense of self:
          the ability to walk alone, when it is necessary;
                    to accept help, when it is needed;
                         and to go on when there is no other way.

I pray that you are blessed with an eternal flame in your soul,
          and that, that light guides you always,
                    from the path of self-destruction
                         to the road of self-fulfillment.

In my prayers ...
          I pray that ...

                    In the midst of darkness, betrayal, pain
                         and exhaustion,

                    Your soul can look high and far,
                         and smile.

Tavion

I will find my strength in you,
            because I could not find it alone.

        That restful place,
        That inner peace,
        That will. That strength.

Searching for the courage to act alone
            I reason - it will be more rewarding
                        than remaining dormant - with companionship.

I am scared of being lonely, lost and forgotten.
So,   I will find my strength in you.

 I have not always done right
            and I have been punished.
 I have not always known the answers,
            so decisions have been made for me.
 I have not always walked forward,
            so I have tripped over past mistakes.

Performing before this audience
            my tears come on cue, my pain is quite genuine
                        but my motions are purely mechanical.

Yet for you I must go on. I *must* be strong.

    So I will find my strength in you.

Throughout the years, I have lost my way
            but, through you ...
                        I have been given a second chance.
                        I have been shown another path
            and through you and your love

            I will find my strength.

Jamie Bear

teeny tiny being
tender toes
slowly fanning

waiting 4 life's winds to blow
anxiously outside
your plastic windows.

I look through, as you rest
cylinder tubes
lie on your chest.

finally, you come home
beautiful boy
never go.

visitors, they daily come
to praise God, and watch
as you blossom.

everyday you amaze
beating the odds
my Baby Brave.

two years and nary a sign
of your plight or
what went thru' medical minds.

then a day I won't forget
a startling reminder
of your early appearance.

as you turn a different hue
struggles to speak
sirens blare to retrieve you.

o 2 mask cups your face
eyes widely staring
images not to be erased.

doctors visits were a few
you laughed & played
everyone 'membered you.

you'd bounce back rapidly,
leading the class,
reading by three.

happy or upset you glowed
commanding attention
our little CEO.

Jamie Bear, tall and slender,
parents' joy
our Boy Wonder.

"Little one, do you eat?
you're so skinny,"
says almost everyone we meet.

You then reply, as mommy directs
"No, I am not.
I am perfect."

The Ball
- TJ

It's hard to guess.
Who's coming?
The future's never clear.

We can't possibly know
Exactly who will show.
Which new guest will now appear?

My mind's drafted several place cards.
Our family's table has been set.
Everyone's ecstatically awaiting the arrival
Of this new, young, prince we have not met.

I imagine your regal entrance.
I hope you feel our warm embrace.
I hope life with us is filled with beauty.
Will you be pleased by how we chose to decorate?

I hope our melodies are to your liking.
I hope each one of us graciously entertains.
I hope our presence brings you comfort.
I hope you grow to cherish your proclaimed name.

As we sit, listening for notable signs
Of your deliverer's sudden approach.
My thoughts begin to gallop forward
To another day that, instantly, feels, too, close.

I foresee that once the music slows
The candlelight flickers, then gradually dims
Sweet, youthful tunes of boyhood
Will become bellowing booms of men.

I pray
You safely arrive quickly
And that future date takes its time.

I will have faith
When my heart travels through memories of soirées together,
Our shared journey will have been divine.

Princess Paws

- Princess Ali

Tiny are the hands of today.
Reaching, seeking
Thru' work, in play.

Counting their fingers.
"1…2...3...4...5!"
Picking prickly blades of grass
Jumping high for the sky.

Tiny are the hands of today.
Pointing, Pinching
Finding their way.

Counting their claps, slowly.
"1…2...3!"
Counting them quickly.
"Mommy, count with me!"

Tiny are the hands of today.
"What's that?"
"Eww…Grandma,
Wipe it away!"

Tiny are the hands of today.
Look at what each hand can do.
"Daddy, can you do this, too?"

Tiny are the hands of today,
Not to be forgotten
"Wait! Brothers, wait!"

So tiny are the hands of today.

But, oh so much more, *BIGGER,*
Than yesterday.

A Salute to Three New Mothers

- jo   - eb

Hunters
From a common ground
We each   took separate paths.
Searching for the roles we'd play
Within this massive cast.

We each had our turns
At conquering fears,
mourning, and losing faith in love.

We stumbled, fell ...
bled more than our shares
Yet fought back   to rise   above.

We waded the storms
and climbed rocky mountains
to set our personalities free.

Now as we mature   live, learn and love
we face our destinies.
With the knowledge of our mothers
and the lessons of our pasts.

In Ms. Angelou's words,
         "**Phenomenal** Women" are we!

We birthed wildflowers in the winter
Most precious of all things
Whom in the midst of our indecision
dangled by their wings.

I know they will be proud of us,
and in turn   see pride in our eyes
At how unexpected visitors
became blessings in disguise.

And on this day
I close my eyes
and clasp my hands in prayer

"I hope you both know
      that wherever you go,
my faith in you is there."

'Lord, Thank You for my sister-friends ...
their children
and my own.
Please help us to reunite one day
and watch
as they grow old.
Help us
to be mothers whom
Within your grace, my King,
can laugh and cry and ease their fears ...
through whatever this world may bring.'

Their Mothers' Sons

Do you think that they will please her
when their day has come?
I hope I've taught, "...respect all women
not just that magic one."

Do you think that they'll remember
when they're out there having fun
to protect her deepest feelings
when all is said and done?

Do you think they'll define beauty
in each and every being?
Creamy chocolate, tannish skin,
blue eyes, straight hair,
            what'll be its meaning?

Do you think that they will fall in love
slow and romantically?
Will they rush to grab forever?
Will they settle and regret it daily?

Or, do you think they will aspire
to covet and to keep
someone who showers them with love
one we will be so proud to meet?

Mileage

I've put so much pressure
on my child
to walk One Hundred
Million Miles.

In my belly,
I did pray
for him to be
The One to save.

At his birth,
I somehow knew
he'd give me strength
in all I'd do.

As a toddler,
I'd proclaim
his artisan
would lead to fame.

Of my young one,
I did stress
for him to make sense
of my mess.

I have put much pressure
on my child
to walk One Hundred
Million Miles.

What I now see
he needs from me
is to love him without exception
and
let him be.

For Our Mommies,

we try to live the lives they've bequeathed us.
As mothers, they always want better for their baby girls.
So, in teaching they've asked us to higher the standards...
to have dreams of a fairytale world.

We are to erase every volatile argument witnessed
and the reconciliation that would then follow.
We are to garnish a suit of armor and
be vigilant when 'Prince Charming' asks to pass through.

We are instructed to omit the familiar
and attempt the unnatural:
To avoid being drawn in by the same type of men
who responded to their calls.

We are to honor our father-figures,
forgive their indiscretions,
respect their roles in our lives
and the humanness of their flawed existence.

Yet, then Mommy instructs in no uncertain terms
that in looking for a mate,
we mustn't choose the way she did.
We mustn't fall for her same bait.

We must somehow make a different choice,
one of which we just can't relate...

"Mommy, ... How?"

"Ay, Dawn"
- *The Birth*

Today, as I touch you
I grant you one wish.

Today, 'fore I leave you
I give you this gift.

The ability to receive
to acquire knowledge
to mislead.

To be cautious. To be frank.
To demolish. To recreate.

To rejoice through tears.
To combat fears.
To look, feel and hear
though your senses disappear.

To call out One Name
and alleviate pain.

To be, think and grow
even when you do not know
which direction you'll flow.

Today, you've been given
the presence of prophecy.

To recognize
(though you may bleed)
intentions and longings,
fallacies and misdeeds
are a part of every being.

*Your gift will allow you **and Me**
to look to the past
and believe
that through all things:
every moment, every dream,
was all, and is to be -
Worth the Living.*

Now.

Breathe.

Phenomenon
Phenomenon

Now

Once,
I knew your name
I read your mind
I shared your thoughts
Completely.

I got on
my knees
I laid on
my back
I permitted you within me.

I nestled your head
Warm in my lap
and lightly
Stroked your ear.

Strong for you
Was I
when things
Got hard
Holding your face
and kissing your tears.

I rose
To your voice
I walked
In your shadow
without realizing the
complications.

I carried out
My duties
as assigned
And was properly armed
for every occasion.

I gave to you
My Being
In it's frailest form
and made you
It's Creator.

Yet when I needed
Time alone
Your response
was always, "Later."

You straightened my back
You gave me a name
You made my voice
Well-versed, like your own.

We fought the same battles
To defend our beliefs
& shared each other's homes.

So when you raised
Your fist to me
It took me
by surprise.
What ever happened
to my lover-friend
And all his Godly Pride.

You spat at me.
You marked my name
And tried
To keep me down.

But somehow figured
through it all
I'd gladly
stick around?

Please
Come to me
With your gallant charm
And do your damnedest
To break My Spirit.

Now,
I recognize you
Clothed or Not
- And welcome you
To attempt it.

You approach me
With your shirt
undone
Your buckle
Fastened loosely

You smile at me
and take my hand
And expect me
To "Go to it."

But I am not that child
Alone and Naïve
without
Knowledge of her Name.

The essence of my life
has become more
Than sharing
In your pain.

Consequences

What if a child had never laughed?
Never saw its parents' clap?

Never heard the words, "I'm proud?"
Deprived of sun. Raised in clouds?

What if that child then grew
To live near me, or near you?

Lacking joy, appreciation, pride.
Filled with anger. Not knowing why.

What if that child then saw,
Their neighbor ... next door?

That child is slowly going MAD,
As they watch you live the life, they wish they had.

What then ...?

Graduation

Every year, I want to cry,
     and plead for their salvation.
With every spring there are *hundreds of thousands*
     filled with mad desperation.

Released unto a world so vast,
     without the proper preparation.
The last four years spent running from Textbook knowledge,
     instead of demanding an education.

Eighteen years of questions, "Who Am I?"
     becoming Rap Masters at the Art of Frustration.
Being punished with detaining sentences,
     and still learning nothing of the Art of Determination.

Y.O.U.

I, too, went to school with welts.
My mother could not control herself.

See in her past
someone thought
      it was wise.
Taught her
to let anger
      be her guide.

Compared to her life,
mine was mild,
        an acceptable way to raise a child.

So, I know that feeling deep inside
That makes you yell, and scream, and cry.

That makes you say, you love them so
and that no one else will ever know
      your struggle.

But you have no right to scar a child.
To make them want to die inside.
To hate themselves and the whole world, too.
To make them never have a clue
      that the problem is really, YOU.

Have you never made mistakes?
Don't *you* know the abused child's fate?
How much more must they take,
Before their hearts begin to break?

    And their expansive minds de-ter-i-or-ate

Because of You.

Children may steal and they may lie.
They may seem cruel,
then they may try
      ...to seek forgiveness.

Honey, there **are** ways to help them learn
that what was done was something wrong.
To feel your love and parental bond,
      ...while strengthening their spirits.

You don't know how?
Well, ask for help!
For THEIR sakes
      ...and for yourself.

You know better than to do
The awful things done to you.

You were the victim once before
YOU yelled, and screamed, and cried, "NO MORE!"

Now, you're the parent.
So, it's O.K.
to treat the powerless that way?

"They drive you crazy," you sometimes say,
and you wish they'd go away.

Well, guess what?
They are here.

And now, they're
Acting Out in fear

Against their teachers and their peers
Against each other and all who are near

and YOU wonder to what it is due?

God has blessed you with the gift of children.
What you are doing *isn't* discipline.
It isn't love or your prerogative.
It isn't fair to this delicate world to give ...

another

Y.O.U.

Walking Blind

I am to them ...
>The exception.
They take solitude
>In making ME different.

They say,
>"You don't know OUR pain."
>"You have not come from where we came."

>"You have not been cursed with our misfortune."
>"You were given so much, and WE, got none."

They say,
>many things to justify
>>their homes, their men ... their lives.
>many things to make it seem
>>they could never live their dreams.
>many things to lessen their parts
>>in the bleeding of their hearts.

I try to uplift
>but they say I preach.

I offer guidance,
>and they say, "Who is *SHE*?"

When they are lacking
>they sit and cry.

When it is given
>there is no reply.

I try to warn them of the invisible wall.
 Tell them, "*He'll* be there when you call."
But they slam into it again and again.
 Never making a single dent.

Never trying to use the door, never trying to use a saw.
Never trying to climb over the top, never trying to just ...

STOP!

I try to warn them that they'll hurt
 tell them, "The next time, it may be worse."
They study their wounds and take a breath
 agreeing a reprieve would be best.

But, after a few days in the sun,
 (once they're somewhat healed) they imagine,
Life ... on the other side of the wall.
 "If I run into it, maybe it'll fall."

Forgetting all past attempts,
 slightly bruised with a gentle limp,
They steady themselves down that hall.
 For another trip to the wall.

The outcome is always the same.
 They feel it's the dream that causes their pain.
Never seeing the top, never seeing the saw,
 never seeing the reachable, unlocked door.

"Open your eyes and you will see,
 that it is not a mystery,
You HAVE been blessed, *SAME* AS ME.
 Or, do you not want ... to be free?"

Pre VIEW

Him?!?!
He drew the winning ticket?
He pulled the longest straw?

His eyes were the most riveting?
His color the most delightful
when mixed and whipped with yours?

Did his aires reveal the future?
Does his breath contain a plan
that aided in your decision to make *HIM*, The Man?

You do know that every habit,
every annoyance, every quirk...
every *GiAnorMous* and *itty bitty*
characteristic
that has the potential
to drive you
BERSERK...

You just injected (*with pleasure*)
into
your body
and
you don't find that
the least bit
ABSURD?!?!

Well...
Now, it's **ALL** yours, forever.
'Cause regardless of what he doesn't
or
he does

You've created another being
who you are obliged
to unconditionally
Love.

So,

      when he tantrums
          ('til he's 30),
      when her teachers delicately call
          (to complain),

      when other parents
      begin to whisper,
when there's no shame
      in their un'earnful gain,

      when the humor
      is overbearing,
      and others give you "the look,"
      and you try to teach them better
      and they couldn't give a hoot,

Remember...
That dude, that you once were glued to?
That completely lacked the ability
to tune in
to social cues?

Yup. Now, that's ALL *you*!

AND...
his constant misspellings,
his phobia of math,
his obsession with his appearance,
his propensity to dwell in the past.

The way he takes the Lord's name in vain.
The way every other word, is profane.

Even the twitch in his eye,
or the one in his hip.

The lack of internal controls.
The way he gnaws his bottom lip.

Or sucks on his tongue.
Or can't swing a bat.
Or can't dunk a ball...
Yup, your kid's got ALL that!

And let's not forget
all she inherited from you.
All those glorious things
You just finally unlearned
how-to-do.

You will relive them
for INFINITY
(times 1, 2, or 3).
Unless,
you make a better decision
about
who and *what*
REALLY
pleases.

Charities

Souls
    with
        no conscience
        no understanding
    skin is a disguise.
What hides beneath?

Eyes that have cried out for sympathy
Mouths shouting in denial
Smiles that hide lies ...

    Pride is not bestowed to those with disadvantages
    It is achieved through struggles to
        overcome them.

Whether it is with a cane
    or with a crutch
    or by crawling

An effort must be made
    before
He can extend his hand to me and say

    My sister   My lover   My partner

    Come With Me.

And I follow him,
    With compassion,
        With respect.

He does not understand that my trust... is a gift of love.

African Aristocrats

Lovely, lovely women,
poised & gracious to a fault.
Feigning interest in me,
though, I fathom it's for naught.

Implausible
they'd see fit
to analyze & critique
when their own burdens are so many,
I'd fancy,
they'd be
more
neighborly.

It must be awfully tiring.
As a matter of fact, I know,
the energy it takes one
to be guarded
& unable to show…

the veracity of your virtue,
the ineludible blemishes we all tote.
Our interests are divergent,
but if we're bridled,
will we ever know?

What is it like to be
as the other?
Not our pretenses,
but what is factual?
Our life experiences may greatly vary
but realize,
we
are
all
still
equals.

VOICES

Profane & vicious banter
Eloquent, but meek
Collusive involuntary chatter
Orchestrated plots as wisdom is seeked.
Overrated rubbish
littered in deceit
Calm and candid executions
affirm motives rattling heat
Stifling gasps for respirations
Violent cries gone unheard
Rumblings of mumbled aspirations
No wonder she is at a loss for words.

Dreaming

Dreams are quite
the "*decept-ors*," I have to say.

For dreams have been known
to take you away.

When the moonlight glistens
in the nighttime sky.

Dreams reveal hidden urges
our alert minds may deny.

The conquests of our slumber
our wake minds overrule.

In the dawning of the morn'
there's a whole 'nother view.

With shut eyes
we dream and dream

fanciful endings
where all live happily.

Temptations unwavering.
The hold is so strong.

The journey thru' Wonder Land
can last all night long.

As the love dust twinkles
our hearts may flip-flop.

Yet, when we awake
it's as if our insides have dropped.

As we arise
we are faced with others' dismay.

For *Dreams* may invade our nights,
but can rarely survive our restless days.

The Shape of Beauty

Softly sloping mountain peaks.
Rippled, rugged, rock-hard heaps.

Criss cross spirals spaciously intertwine.
Curvaceous planes form luscious lines.

Swirls and swerves,
Slopes and curves.

Spirals, planes, valleys and peaks

Shape not beauty
        like oval orbs

as they Look, Love and Beam!

Senses

Never again will I feel so great
for such little things with sly intentions,
luring eyes,
and meaningless advances.

Will time teach me to trust, what I feel?

Love

Curiosity births an unmistakable fondness
and it grows from there.
There develops complex feelings
for those whom you can trust
and share.

Boredom

Boredom makes the clock stop,
the ocean still, and laughter cease.
There is a feeling of weariness
Yet you strive to stay awake
If only for the simple fact that things might
just get better.

Satisfaction

Satisfaction is...
a gorgeous white,
shone light bright,
through a mahogany crescent.

Comfort

Comfort is...
feeling his little head
baby soft
his breath on your skin
his chest rising and lowering
his fisted arms stretching out
witnessing the corner of his mouth
as it slowly
forms a smile
that tells you
his dreams
> are filled
>> with peace.

Peace

Peace is ...

knowing

that

each

and

every

morning

HE

will

be there...

The Perfect Being

You see what I see
and you hear what I hear.
You know what I mean,
even when I'm unclear.
You feel what I feel
(and know that it's real).
You look to resolve
 and not to repeal.
You see, you hear,
 you feel and you know
'cause you take the time
to learn and to grow.
You find ways ... to value me
even when you disagree.
You share your beliefs
and disappointments, respectfully.
You look to me (faithfully)
to give you what you need.
And when you look,
what you see
Is another
Perfect Being.

The Perfect Being in Me

I see what you see
and I hear what you hear.
I know what you mean,
even when you're unclear.
I feel what you feel
(and know that it's real).
I look to resolve
 and not to repeal.
I see, I hear,
 I feel and I know
'cause I take the time
to learn and to grow.
I find ways ... to give of me
even when I disagree.
I share my beliefs
and disappointments, respectfully.
I look to you (faithfully)
to give me what I need.
And when I look,
what I see
Is another
Perfect Being.

Flames
Flames

Part 1
Part 1

Enlisted

Damn it, I'm so angry
'bout what you've gone and done.
Yes, I'd rather you work in a kitchen
than to lose *us* before we've begun!

Maybe, I am selfish.
I know that you feel lost.
Does that mean at this young age
you vow to die for an unknown cause?!

I will not stand beside you.
I can not, it's not right.
Do you realize this is permanent?
Baby, you have pledged our life.

A Childless Father.

His Child.

His child breathes the breath of God
Conception: due to our union
A likeness that is so much his.
He has had an effect.

He did not stick by him
or support me.
He did not provide for him
or protect me.
He did not work for him
or work with me.

I look at the resemblance
everyday
and remember the stories
told of a family that would fill
an infant's face
with peaceful smiles.

A dream that words told
would only come true
with everlasting, unquestioning
belief in a man;
who though he loved a boy
who reflected his childhood innocence and my eyes
and displayed a smile that drew an adoring crowd,

He could not feed nor clothe,
visit nor care for him.

Because
though words told,
he loved this boy
with every breath,

after nine months and one year
of empty promises to the contrary,
the man had come to the conclusion
that he did not know how to be
and did not want to be...

A Father.

So, earning less income than this man,
still going to school
and receiving no financial,
emotional,
or anyway otherwise,
assistance from this man,

I learned to be one.

Your Child

He breathes the breath of God.
His Conception: due to our union.
His likeness
reflecting your childhood innocence.

You have had an effect.

An effect which ended
The day
You forgot him.
Yet, our dream has been realized:
He lives a life of peace
and he smiles.

A smile that draws an adoring crowd
one that frames eyes that are of my likeness
and reflects nothing
of you
and your weakness.

Kiss, Kiss

Knock ... Knock ...
Who's there?
Oh, you ... again.
I'm sorry, I'm sorry, I can't let you in!

I know you have changed.
I have heard it before.
I forgive you, O.K.
Just please leave my door.

You ask, "Don't I miss you? Do I love you?
            Don't I care?"
I will tell you.   I do.   I will always.
            But I'm scared.

I have given you chances.
I offered you my heart.
I tried to build us a family,
            but you tore it apart.

There were too many excuses;
            too many "I can't"'s and "I will"'s,
but you never did.
It was left to me
            to pay the bill.

I tried to listen,
            to see things through your eyes.
I hurt you when we were younger,
            that I will not deny.

But I am different now, the mother of your child
            or don't you know?
I must work two jobs in order to provide
            the things that you won't.

I admit that in the beginning
    you acted like a man.
But even then, you couldn't commit
    and in the end ... you ran.

You came here, for what?
Are you lonely again?
Have your playmates all left you?
Are you tired of your friends?

I AM NOT like the others.
I AM a strong Black woman
    with pride
Intelligent enough not to allow you to use me
    for a free ride.

No.
I am not hateful.
God has eased my vengeful heart.
I am still healing, but our son needs me
And for him, I have made a new start.

As you can see,
we do not need you
and when you come
    you never offer much more.

So, please do not come knocking
    at our door anymore.

The Chase

I met him under circumstances
that were neither unusual, nor rare.
I did not see him as a mate
or the two of us as a pair.

Yet, his intellect enthralled me.
His patience was surreal.
I tried my hardest to deny it,
forcing myself not to stare.

But often my eyes would wander
My imagination giving chase
I somehow happened upon this land of his
One that my mind can never erase.

We sat and talked for hours.
His dimpled grin lit up the room.
I felt myself unwinding
But knew I would have to be leaving soon.

He looked at me so sadly
And slightly rose my head.
He took my hand so gently
and squeezed it as he said,

"I do not know why you hide
or what it is you seek,
but in my land you are a Queen
and freely you can speak."

When daylight came
the King and I
were ourselves again.
The night had gone
And so, too, had my dreaming
haltered to an end.

But then one day
I looked at him
and was held captive by his eyes.
I visualized his body rising
up and down
between my thighs.

I have tried to stop the visions.
Direct my thoughts in other ways.
And though I have succeeded in keeping my distance,
I desire him more and more each day.

Love Isn't...

Once upon a time,
a young girl had a special friend.
He showered her with lavish praise
and unheralded attention.

Mornings, he would greet her
with a very unique gift:
a folded piece of newsprint
with words that read, *Love is...*

Each she would treasure.
Keep safe for many years.
Until the day their memory
would evoke too many tears.

She thought,
"Did we ever read them?"
Couldn't possibly be so.
'Cause all of what love is...
neither of them showed.

Love isn't...
a haunting feeling
that you're doing something wrong.
Being granted stolen instances
that make nights forever long.

Love isn't...
always wondering
if today or tonight he'll call.
Cradling the receiver
fearing he may never dial at all.

Love isn't ...
being breathless
at every sudden ring.
It isn't never knowing
what each moment will bring.

Love isn't …
quickly raging,
feeling crazed and insane
when unable to talk to him
or hear him speak your name.

Love isn't …
being unfiltered,
being together, wildly free.
It isn't ignoring reality
or other liabilities.

Love isn't…
helping him fantasize
that you are by his side.
It isn't sitting, idly waiting,
for the least inopportune time.

Love isn't…
having to question
what it is or what it isn't.
It isn't ruminating
on what he said or what you didn't.

Love isn't…
uncontrollable compressions
squeezing at your chest.
It isn't compiling somber love songs
deciding which suits you best.

Love isn't … his definition.
Love isn't … as you've defined.
      And the more time passes, you *must* realize
Love isn't something
    you and he
        will ever
           together
             find.

Seraph

I am still learning to live without you.
I remember the love that we once shared.
It was supposed to be you and me forever
Now I must train myself **not** to care.

I can not go on reaching out to you
when on your side the attempts are so few.
How long does it take to be ready?
For you to finally make your move?

You say you are afraid to disappoint
and you weren't prepared to be a father.
What should I do now with that information?
Just wait until it's ok for you to be bothered?

How can you possibly love us,
but live day after day without placing a call?
How can I be the love of your life
when you couldn't give our relationship your all?

I know you must blame me for wanting out.
There is much I do not understand.
I *want* to believe you "want more" and accept
"it's been a struggle being a young Black man."

I have so many questions to ask you,
but maybe I don't want the reasons why.
Who am I to demand answers? Besides
there is no reason that could quiet my cries.

There *are* those times I wonder
if it's possible for a person to care any less.
Then I stop and remember the man
who replaced that emptiness.

There is a man who provides an example -
        the importance of faith in a Being above.
Who has given his own freedom to protect
the innocent little life you refuse to love.

There is a man who has somehow made
the burden in my heart a little lighter.
A man who has worked really hard
at being an incredible father.

There is a man who was right there before me.
A man that I can't help but love.
He has awoken my senses, helped me dream big
and has gradually earned my trust.

There is a man who has taken a chance on love,
who has taught us both to survive
who tucks him in night after night,
rocking him back to sleep when he cries.

Yes, there is a man who follows Our Guide
who's risen every Sunday to receive God's word
His life is directed by His light
I know to you that thought must sound absurd.

But there is a young Black man
who is every bit as afraid,
but wants this life and love too much
he can not run away.

He watched on in amazement
as our only son learned to speak
And he explains to him those challenging issues
only a strong man can teach.

I am not sure what all this means
for you, and for I.
There are still many, *many* moments
when I reflect on our old life.

(I feel so thrown and though) I am still struggling
with how to completely let you go.
What I *am* certain of, is God sends us angels
to show us our intended road.

The Staple

Ugh!

It is the staple.
It is the smallest portion of my frustration
Yet it seems the most persistent.

Unlike the others, who with the increase and decline
of opportunity and circumstance
fluctuate
in their tendency to annoy and perplex,
IT, is transfixed.

It is like the staple which appears to hold
everything together
so nice and orderly.

Yet when removed
not only has its own shape been badly tarnished
but it has left its mark:
      permanent scars
      penetrating holes
      irreparable traces
           of its existence and inexistence
that no amount of corrective measures can disguise.

He is that staple.

Though he has been removed,
I can not mask the impact he's had on my life.

The holes are so miniscule, yet impossible to fill.
The scars have all faded but will not disappear.
The memories, traces of his existence,
have been systematically driven from the day,
but periodically, subconsciously, appear
      during the night...

Turning Back
Turning Back

Guilty Pleasures

I stopped hating you
When I stopped needing you
    as my own.

Not needing you
I again see you
As you are ... alone.

Seeing you
I again value you
I respect you
I miss you.

Missing you
I desire to have you
    With me.

With me
You strive to please me.
I strive to lift us.
We love too deeply.

Do you understand now

Why I can't see you
Hear you
    Be near you?

Together
The burden buries us
    Completely.

I fear you:
To desire you
To need you
To again hate you.

Hating you,
I know you will never again

Be my own.

Understand

His Daddy was a young man.
A beautiful, sweet, young fine man,
never flaunting or wanting a dime man.

Though they lived far apart
he gave of his heart.
Unfortunately, his heart could not feed a hungry man.

Turning Back

You made such awesome choices.
You sacrificed your role.
I used to hate you for it.
Now, I realize you were bold.

It couldn't have been easy
(although, it lessened your load).
How can I now fault you?
'Cause you did what you were told?

What else were you to do?
How could you understand?
Yes, I expected much from you
but not to give in to *every* demand.

I wanted you to fight harder.
I needed you to care.
To tell me there's no way in hell
that you could ever bear...

to be pulled away & separated from
the one thing you *did* love.
I needed you to believe (what I couldn't)
That, *him*, you **were** worthy of.

LONGINGS

Longing for what we could not reach
but fought our best to grasp.
Memories of your gentle lips
and your infectious laugh.

Wanting to be a staple for you
as you have been for me.
Wishing that it's beyond your control
and that I, too, invade your dreams.

So, when I call and say,
'it's your voice I miss and wish to hear,'
it's also our first promise of forever
which has stayed with me through the years.

A Lifetime of Love
- cls

At the end of your journey
I hope you continue
     to love me.

At the end of my journey
I hope time allows me
     to remember.

Remember
what is so paramount
     that I now forget.

The memory of our moment.

I loved you blindly,
     sweetly,
          painstakingly
              and deeply.

And there continues to be
     parts of me
          still in love with you.

Moving On

Losing *me* nearly killed him.
See, our bond was so strong.
But, somehow, he recovered and was able to move on.

I wonder 'bout the process
'cause he never wrote, nor called.
I remember waiting for the ring
But, somehow, he'd moved on.

He vowed to never love another
I was his family, he'd reclaim.
He'll have to divide his time, as I wait in line,
'cause somehow he's moved on.

It's hypocrisy, I know. I have always wished him well.
I have treaded another course...so what,
if he's moved on as well?

He says, he'll...love me...forever
and thoughts of me still turn him on.
But every night he lies down at *her* side
and is able to move on.

I am being somewhat covetous
maybe soon *these feelings will have gone*.
'cause emotions, though overflowing,
mustn't ever stop *me* ... from moving on.

Clouded

My insecurity
has somehow led me
to feel and to see
things that in actuality
have not been placed before me.

It's funny, what we perceive,
what we assume will one day be

What will you guarantee?

What is it I believe…
will come from such risky…?
I can not afford to proceed
without some type of warranty.

Hypothetically speaking
exactly
what is it
that
you'd be
offering?

Traps

L ively
Laughing

    Always mapping

    Making plans
    to be MY MAN

T ouching
Taunting

    Always fawning

    Over what
    we COULD NOT HAVE

W isely
Wording

    Handsome, Charming

    Skillful with your
    large, long hands

S moothly
exting

Never failing

Memories of
a *ravenous* past.

W hispers
ake me

Your voice takes me

to that warm, wet
perilous blast

W ould you
orry

if I hurried?
Responding, "Yes. Let's run away."

C ould we
apture

Our Lost Forever

if all we can promise
one another
is

today?

The Ghosts of "Forever and Always"

Transforming a lover
      Into a friend
Has been up until now
Just an illusion.

      Unable to find where the process begins
      or where past feelings abruptly end.

Suddenly, it appears, he wins.
For I have, by chance, discovered a way to amend
what was once untameable burning passion.

Unexpectedly, though, it appears that it's *him*
my mind's transformed into 'this friend.'

In my heart there is something between you and I
that remains raw:

You have held and never relinquished
my core.

So now you know what haunts and tortures
my soul...

I fear, it has *always* and will *forever*
be *yours*.

Waking

visions are alarming
dreams seem real
holding tightly to the image
not defining its appeal

should have... been reticent of these queries
... known it wouldn't take too long
curious, I never wished to be her?
just felt she didn't *(in our equation)* belong

his continuous devotion
was my momentary escape
as well, an unconscious reminder
of why I vacated her space

the reasons I disembarked
washed away with the hate
i could no longer see our conflicts
or relive the effects of my mistakes

damn, I keep ending up here
no matter how or what I try
Cold & Distant, Warm & Open
or "...So Hot" as he describes

i am no one special
not to him, *although he says,*
in the absence of our presence
he'll be with some other face?

i am no one's mistress
although with him it's how I behave
if he loved me, truly loved me
would he have me take that place?

Why do I reach out to him?
Why do I still for him, wait?
What disturbed my ignorant indifference?
Why must I *still*, with him, love or hate?

Help Me

How can we start over
go back a week or two
to that initial conversation
when I asked, "How are u?"

Can we travel back in time
before we crossed so many lines,
before I pretended you were mine
and professing love for me was fine?

Before we flipped that mental switch?
Before that 1st imagined kiss?
Before you proposed I touch my hips
and I envisioned your strong grip?

Before you asked, "where 2 put it?"
and 'fore I then described in depth:
"...in my mouth, between my lips,
along my tongue and fingertips."

Right before you asked to see
a picture showing *all of me?*
Right before, I agreed
then wondered if the image pleased...

Back before the very start?
Before the chance to crumble hearts?
Prior to our plans to dart
across the world to embark

on a road so very dim?
Me hiding all these things from him.
And from her, you also hid,
her, my replacement in your bed.

At one time, she was me.
U and him? Duality.

Desires are worth destroying these?!?!?!
What will it take to let this be?

Can we both together approve,
or will the changes displease you?

This request not meant to confuse.
I would just somehow like a *Redo.*

How can *we* once more begin?
Can we play the start again?
Can we press rewind *and then*,
        ...can we ever be *just* friends?

PUPPETEER

Cords Pulled
Ropes Burn

He rises…
Now…it's my turn.

Volunteered this mind
At his command

To allow him rule
No questions asked.

Taking place
letters rearranged

New: *Conductor*
Stage…Unchanged.

The Mirror

We must, in some way, differ.
He and I can't be the same.
He has been *repeatedly* unfaithful.
It's just my mind that should be ashamed.

I can, will, and do, judge him.
He allowed his body to stray.
I have let no other, *physically*, enter
Although, I admit the line is gray.

He really should know better.
I have been trying to cut the ties.
He has established another household
I told one, two, *maybe* three white lies.

There *must* be a difference.
To say and do is something else.
I would never follow his example.
He forever betrayed my trust.

We must, in some way, differ.
He and I *can't* be the same.
If a pattern is embedded
then it is *he* that I blame.

Villainess

"We are done!"
"It is over!"
I keep saying we are through.
"You are not right for me
and I am so bad for you."

One of us must be the villain.
Bid the other one adieu
This can't go on forever.
Come on, just do it, make this move.

I am staring in this mirror
reviewing all the rules,
counting those we've broken
rehearsing how to conclude.

Just say it, "It is over."
I mean it, I really do.
Someone has to finally end it.
Maybe, that someone could be you?

Trials

TRY
LISTEN
TAKE
PAUSE.

Our existence
has a cause,
...and a cost.
Many pay
for every day
and each mistake.

Truth?
Who viewed
Wisdom's Lot

and knew
that I'd
forget-them-not?

Treachery
Deceit
Vanity
Plain Ole' Greed.

Look.
Now.
Think
I've gone mad?

Trade with *you*
All that
you've grabbed.
Then, *I* may play
A *Different* Hand.

Closure

Each time we meet
      we prepare to say goodbye.

How can a relationship plagued with dead ends
      ever stand the test of time?

Our emotions are ever-changing.
      We are eternally editing scripts.

There are so many revised editions.
      Why *can't I just accept The End...*
            ... as it is?

Flames
Flames

Part 2
Part 2

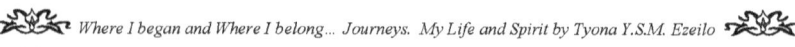

The Two

There are many missions in our lifetime.
Many objects to pursue.
There's that endless quest for riches.
Tarnished treasures to renew.

My quest is never ending.
I've been born time and time again.
I've loved you, and I've hated you.
Only to love you, yet again.

Two hearts have felt mine's passion
And our connection never ends:
The broken man, I've called my lover.
The faithful man, I've called my friend.

Soul Ties

Can you feel me calling
deep within your soul?
Can you hear my whispers
calling you home?

Binded by my ego.
Twisted is our love.

The beauty of love-making -
unions blessed from up above -

Tainted by our motives.
Contaminated is the dove.
Thorned & wilted roses
polluted by mistrust.

Roped into submission.
Naked and Ashamed.
Marked for exhibition,
branded with each other's names.

Do you feel our burden?
Is the struggle clear?
Will the knots of our endeavors
ever disappear?

Survival

Hidden in the darkest
places of my heart.
When asked, am I happy?
I struggle to remark.

Havens overcrowded
Alliterated with trickling tears
Passion's purpose 'pears forgotten
Perhaps, withered by passing
Years.

The rounded apples of my cheekbones,
converted into pears.

The wide white eyes full of promise,
barren and unclear.

The pink plump lips pursed for battle
...censored by fear

Or maybe by conditioning - why speak
to those who fail to hear?

Am I happy? - never answered.
               (At least not truthfully so).
He asks for validation,
he doesn't really care to know.

I hide for protection – correction -
I hide to *feel* safe.
I hide for when I reveal myself,
he shows me his disdain.

And so, I remain hidden
in the Darkest Places of my heart,
repeating, "he truly does love *most* of me

as long as I hide the other parts."

At the Core

No. You are no less than I.
Still, I must remember, no more.
This is not a war.
No one is keeping score.

I want to give my love
but I am so scared.
It feels like a dare …
and there is so much

      my mind

      &

      body

already bear.

Explaining My Silence

Since when did I become someone to ridicule,
belittle and speak down to?
God, it becomes so difficult to again feel
a valued, respected, part of you.

What happened to the passion?
Where has my desire gone?
I expected things to change
but not to feel so alone.

The dreams I wish to live
I can not get you to believe.
I can't keep up with how I've let you down.
I just can't seem to please.

Do I begin again?
Do I forgive and forget?
Do I pretend I am your all,
then pray hard that we'll make it?

Do I keep on make-believing
that it all pleases me
that I am happy and content
then pray hard for it to be?

I am not your perfect partner -
That in your eyes I see.
I am far less than you hoped for,
and none of that is o.k. with me.

But don't I deserve, "I am sorry?"
Aren't I worthy of apologies?
Do I just giggle and release it
and try to make my**self** feel free?

You tell me, 'Help, **we** do <u>not</u> need"
because it's **me**, not *you*.
Was that said in the heat of the moment?
Or were you, **then,** speaking your truth?

I am bombarded with these questions
and paralyzed with fear.
Why has my heart quit listening?
Will I ever stop questioning what I hear?

I separate myself from you
and the tension is released.
I no longer question my self-worth
and begin to love who I see.

Why **is** that?
How could it be?
If I was **meant** for you
and you *intended* for me?

Being blessed with such gifts,
a life that others envy,
why can't I satisfy you
or receive the love that **I** need?

I have not given up hope
or given in to doubt,
but I have no more solutions.
Just can't figure us out.

So, I walk around in silence.
Although, I love you, endlessly.
The thought of confrontation is so deadly,
and silence, so easy.

LIMITS *(My 2 cents)*

If my heart were so big
that I could not hate
(for even those who disappoint
my love would be great)

If we could not share
a common enemy
and all those you despise
were a friend to me.

Would you forever and ever
feel betrayed by me?

If my quest for happiness
were fueled by relentless drive.
If I based my success and
"good"ness
on how hard I tried.

If we could not see
quite eye to eye
as to what
was "just enough" of a supply

Would you begin to believe
that I could never
be satisfied?

If I failed you somehow
...and then, again.
After you repeatedly asked
that it not happen.

If I could not comply
with set conditions
and I told you, "I must be
My Own Person"

Would you conclude
you must now choose
a more suitable
woman?

If you exposed all your flaws
and I revealed my sins.

If it were known that parts are strong
and others weakened.

If your mind exploded
with valid reasons
and ways to justify
your situation(s)

If my eyes (for you) harnessed *only*
compassion,
would yours (for me) stand in
judgment?

Would you harshly condemn *only*
my indiscretions?

If promised to one another
for eternity...

Could anything ever tear you
away from me?

?

SPARRING

We haven't worked out, all, the kinks.
Our missteps have been more than a few.
You are just beginning to know me
and I still can't read your cues.

We've danced this dance before.
I remember, it was you!
I think, back then, I took the lead...
you kept stepping on my shoes.

The music was so rapid.
We couldn't keep the beat.
It felt like everyone was watching,
so we danced on, merrily.

I was barely breathing
and you kept checking the time.
Nevertheless, we danced on.
What was going through your mind?

Hmm, what was I thinking?
I know I was anxious for the song to end.
When it did, we parted ways...
Yet, here we are, again.

Answers

If I could just STOP
From needing, *me*
And instead opt
To be happily married

How freeing would it be?

If I could forget
Yesterday's trip
Gut my mind
And walk blindly behind

How very charming would he, again, seem?

If I bit my tongue
Until it bled
While visions of days of fun
Scrolled through my head

Would I never again be the source of dread, according to
he?

If I consistently sought permission,
Did only what I was told,
And my opposition
Never showed,

Would that be enough to please?

I could take
More on my plate
And never make
Another mistake
Never need a single break,
Or need for him to commiserate,

Maybe, THAT would change our fate?

If I grew three more boobs,
And sprouted wings,
And invented a money chute,
And my Va-jay-jay sang,

Would I then be considered a valuable thing?

If I could stop
Reaching the top,
And if my roll began to slow,
Revealing no more, the things I know,

Would I no longer be threatening?

If balancing scales
Was no longer my hobby,
If I realized measuring fails
Can never be done properly,

Would that be enough to revive, 'we'?

If I...
If I...
If I's...
Could overtake my life,
And when I die
He'll simply say, 'goodbye!'
And then, he'll find
A replacement 'I.'

Holiday

One day I will discover
that I
am better than this

and the world
as he's come to know it
will cease to exist.

I will find my sanity
and take the necessary steps

to correct my situation
and to live as I see fit.

Again?

Forgive me that I hurt you.
Forget that I was so wrong.
Recall the times I touched you.
It hasn't been that long.

Imagine how I struggled.
Know I want to erase your pain.
Give me a chance to do better...
I will take all the blame.

Let me make a difference.
Allow me to repent.
What will restore your trust in me?
Provide me the slightest hint.

With that I will make you see
that this is <u>not</u> the end.
You just have to give me one more chance -
just *one* more chance, again.

Visiting

Only I can take me back there.
Down the path from which I came.
It is I, who pulls the trigger,
leaving me wounded, making me lame.

No one else is liable.
I have no puppeteers.
It is I who dons the garment.
The guilty conscience that I wear.

I know not to return there.
The result is never good.
Briefly, I do revel
but it doesn't mean I should.

Hearing voices summon,
knowing no one else is listening,
I try to justify my deeds
stating I am only visiting.

Lost

Lost

I spoke of once
not knowing
Who I was
or Where I'd go.

I never could've
imagined
it would be *worse*
one day, to know.

Expanse

As we sensed
a storm
approaching

As you watched
clear skies
shift to gray

As I felt
the BOOM
of thunder

Somehow
Someway
we made   space.

FORTUNE

You... knew that it would happen.
You saw it in my eyes.
Was it when I breathed in my 1st breath?
Or, when I exhaled my 1st cry?

You feared the teller's warnings
while holding back your pride.
You yearned to rejoice in all we'd promised,
but felt we'd one day... welcome... good-bye.

I LOVE...

foolish women
hide their treasures
worship trinkets
polish trash

giddy girlies
speak of lost loot
they discarded in the past

silly secrets
they once whispered
broadcasted, (such is news)

once wise choices
now mistaken
for doing
anything
they choose.

uncontrollable sensations
bright & blissful smiles
deep & distant gazes
disconnected
from their worlds

quivers of excitement
shivering when not alone
hoping no one knows
their longing
to bring stolen treasures
home

I ...
Long to clench my treasures
Open padded rooms again
Very quickly peek inside them
Even step inside again

I...
Live to tell those secrets
Of the golden story books
Versions very deeply buried in
Every copy he once took

wishing I did not *crave* them
wishing I'd realize, it's too late
wishing I did not *need* them
wishing my heart could lock its gates
wishing they didn't move me
wishing I could forget their shine
wishing I didn't hear them call me
wishing I could accept...
they are **_NOT_** mine.
wishing I *wasn't* foolish
wishing I couldn't feel
wishing I did not know their beauty
wishing that, for me...they'd no appeal
wishing I'd live in the present
wishing I'd forget the past
wishing I knew that giddy girlies
must realize fairytales... *never* last

those who worship trinkets
those who revel in past loves
those who can't control their longings
those who covet others' doves...

my body tremors as I think of them
How do those stories end?

What becomes of ...*foolish* women?
woo'ers of **men**?

foolish women
see the tremble
of my hands
and quickly state,

"If you truly
love
Your Golden Treasures
you **must** pack
them
all
away."

Nervous Neurons.

Stop!

Don't sing.
Don't talk.
Don't look.
Don't pout.

Ok, breathe.

If you must......but not in the house!

DEEP

Didn't know it mattered.
Never had a clue.
Didn't know that can of worms
Contained a glob of glue.

Didn't read the label.
Guess I didn't care.
Yep, opened up that can, and now,
My mess is everywhere!

Everywhere I look,
Can't escape that can!
Clean-up's been a pain in the ass -
The crap even hit the fan!

Perhaps,
next time that I open one...

I'll pay more attention to where it might land.

I Under-Estimated Love

*I could not have then foreseen
how **crucial** it would be
to define:
what it meant to **me***

To Be Loved.

*Maybe, passion wasn't **IT.**
Maybe, hearts don't always skip.
Maybe they only skip a bit.*

Who then knew?

*Perhaps, he needed **not** be schooled?
Maybe it's o.k. to act a fool.
Maybe, there are no steadfast rules.*

I had   —no-   clue!

Love.

*Was it falling for its traps?
Being naïve, going back?
Was it visiting places that hold pain?
Traveling there, again and again*

searching... for love?

*Was it accepting borrowed time?
Ignoring all the lies?
Losing my mind?
Oh, and all the hours crying...*

in need ... of love?

My Love...?

Nana's full strong arms,
soft, warm, shielded from threats of harm.

Mommy's nervous gaze
watching with pride, as her child takes the stage.

One, vulnerably stating things,
that alone, one, also, seems to mean.

That

- is what –

I LOVE.

It is the one who knows me.

The one who sees my humanity:

> *the Wolf and the Lamb,*
> *the Hero and the Fan,*
> *my flesh and my soul,*
> *and many things*
> *I've never told*

> *My Lover knows.*

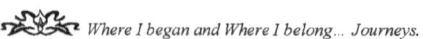

...questioning things

What does it mean
When words mean...
  Not a Damn Thing,
   To me?

How could it Be?
Who removed me...
  From all that could,
   Move me?

HOW could it be?
Who de-sense-i-tized me
  To all that would
   excite me?

Why can't I cry?
Would I have told that lie
  If I could
   Hear me?
What does it mean?

What does it mean?

What sensations describe touch?
Which tastes crave ME too much?
What message does the evening rain bring?
To Me...Not a Damn Thing!

Have I evolved?
Is THIS the "real" world?
Do <u>all</u> wise men wear a veil?
Have they learned how words fail?

Where do words now hide?
How can they disguise
    The Power and the Pain,
    The desperation and the rage...

      That once dwelt
      in me?

<u>Can</u> I still write?
Do a pen and paper still provide
    Refuge and Release
    Absolution and PEACE
      From what <u>still</u>
      Disturbs me?

How in the midst of <u>madness</u>
Does one create?

How? How?!
And not b-r-e-a-k...

What does it mean?!

What does it mean!

What...does this mean?

Exits

Possibly, it was not meant
Perhaps, a shift of intent

Given the benefit of doubt
Helps to find a way out

Or uncover a way in
A place to again, begin

Steps are being laid
Progress? Made?

It is so much of the same
Repetitive, painful game

Not sure I want my name
To still be Mrs. All-to-Blame

So, how to escape?
To stop trying to replace

The holes in his sight
To stop trying to be right

To stop attempting to lead
Or restructure personalities

To contain the tools & keys
To live a life of wisdom, and maturity.

I am not a saint
Tired of checking my mate
Need to nurture, Me
And become all that was foreseen.

Do not want to hide, or
Participate in vicious fights.
I've devoured my pride,
And now I wonder, why?

MY PLAN...

*I'm going to make this thing **HAPPEN**.*

In whichever way I can.

*I'm going to make this thing **HAPPEN**.*

I'm not waiting on this man.

*I'm going to make this thing **HAPPEN**.*

*I'm workin' on a **MASTER** plan.*

*I am going to make this thing **HAPPEN**.*

And don't need anyone to hold my hand.

PROCESSING ME

Do I believe in me?
Do I realize what you've seen?
Do I know I've touched a soul?
Have I helped you reach your goals?

I don't know.

Will I invent again?
Will I reconnect with old friends?
Will I regret all I've told?
Have I somehow changed my world?

I don't know.

Am I all I should be?
Am I enough for my family?
Am I just a chick who thinks in rhymes?
Have I wasted my time?

I don't know.

I need to share what I feel
I need to feel that you hear
I need to hear I'm not alone
Then, I *hope* to grow...
...to know.

Where I began and Where I belong... Journeys. My Life and Spirit by Tyona Y.S.M. Ezeilo

Casualties
Casualties

199

The Death of .....

interrupted parents
interrupted sons
interrupted daughters
interrupted fun.

interrupted artists
interrupted breaths
interrupted geniuses
interrupted rest.

interrupted thoughts and dreams
stories yet to unfurl
interrupted lovers

in an all too interrupted filled world.

Have You Ever Seen Your Face In a Casket?

Have you ever felt the presence of a spirit?

Have you ever refused to believe?

Have you ever slept & dreamt that it wasn't?

Have you ever thought, "It could have been me?"

Have you ever seen your face in a casket?

Have you ever tried to hold on 'til the end?

Have you ever really known and lost a true love?

How do you cope with the death of a friend?

Quiet Spirits ... I think of you

*The children I have buried
in unmarked tombs
are the children who trusted
that in my womb
they'd find sanctity & serenity
from the teratogens
that sought out with villainous vengeance
to dissemble them.*

*Would their tiny hearts have filled with sadness
if they had foreseen...
the one true terror to their awaiting liveliness
as me?*

Whispers Rock My Child to Sleep
-Nana

It's traveled long distances and in It creeps,
to rock my weary child to sleep.

It cloaks her with Its lukewarm winds
as she hesitantly welcomes Him,

to seal her eyes and calm her heart
to travel in dreams to where it's never dark.

They rest so far and though I cannot see
I've been told They have rested my child in Peace.

Words So Simple

She lives with words so simple.
She never seems to care.

He tells her that work beckons him,
but isn't really there.

She's running out of options.
She gives until it hurts.

He's bounded by second chances,
but cannot give her what she's worth.

She releases him from bondage.
She declares him to be free.

He asserts his independence
as she maintains her surety.

She lives with words so simple,
and adopts a covenant to retain.

She'll forget she ever knew him,
but her heart recalls the pain.

Riddled

One day, I awoke
and realized
I was
powerless.

That day,
I splintered into selves
who require
less maintenance.

> Operating for attention.
> Forced to submit.
>
> *That day,*
> I gave my beauty
> and gave up
> all my innocence.

Fallen angels about me.
Resolution not readily retrieved.

That day,
I let free my reliance
on life's simplest
securities.

> Wanting to love. Suddenly seeing
> I can't convince him to provide.
>
> *That day,*
> I extracted all my plans
> to live forever
> by his side.

Sharing every weakness.
He used them, *every*, one.

From *that day*,
I ignored cordial words
and believed *only*
his actions.

Unforeseen conditions
Blistering threats

That day,
I expelled God's first sign
he could bring me
happiness.

Humbled & grief-stricken,
I was cast away.

That day,
I packed up my belief
he was sent to me -
to save.

Ailments and afflictions,
worsening, in a spirited icon.

That day,
I promptly erased the need
and accepted the mother I had,
had gone.

Angry & disappointed,
pointing out my struggle for the kids to see.

That day,
I vowed to never forget
he's capable of poisoning them
against me.

Eyes that claim to love me
spewing so much hate.

That day,
I changed forever.
Every joyous feeling
I'd now debate.

Painfully reflecting,
seeing all the heartache that's been bred.

That day,
I released my last tear.
There was no more left
to shed.

In an instant it quickly hit me.
Perhaps, I knew it to be true.

I *had* been slowly broken
and never fully renewed.

There are pieces of me
floating
out there
in the atmosphere

and ***that day***
(I fear is near)
when I will have all
but *disappeared...*

Mercy

Sometimes, it's not just
what you have
or *how* you've planned
or *when* you land…
it's *where*
and with *whom*
you
 STAND.

Again, I've watched
an angel fly
(one who soared
long before she died)

Some days, we live
our lives, alone.

Some days, we share
with all who've flown.

Tributes
Tributes

I Do

I sit here and I watch him
laying valiantly in this bed.
Listening to him make small talk,
avoiding my eyes, sensing the dread.

This cannot be happening.
"Oh, please, God, please heal my husband.
Let him make it through this surgery
and witness the arrival of his new son.

Let the tests reveal it's nothing.
Let him so quickly recover.
Let this be just one of those things
that challenge us but, we get over.

I know I haven't been grateful
(as I really need to be)
that you have sent this special man
to be for only me.

I know I must do better and
will make an effort every day
to love and to cherish
        (in health as in sickness)
the life you save today."

My Sister

Ready to defend me in a brawl
Standing by my side all of 4 ft. tall.

Fights with the dishcloth.
Throwing each other over the couch
Screaming and biting and cursing aloud.

Helping me make music videos for school.
Doing the wop and just swearing she's cute!

10-years-old,
Rolling her eyes with hands on her hips
Kicking out my boyfriends
Who called her "a trip."

Cheering me up and making me smile.
I always had a partner to act crazy and wild.

Winking her eye and blowing a kiss
A camera's flash she'll never miss.

5 foot 8 inches tall and 100 lbs. thin
Cocoa complexioned skin
Rarely seen without a grin

My Sister

Her glowing presence never did I appreciate
'till she left on her first date.
Things will never be the same
Adolescent popularity has staked its claim.

Whatever happened to that ever-present pain?

My Sister

My Aunts

There are these women that I know
who always humbly seem to show
        to me
              their glory.

Women on each side
who have been with me throughout my life.

These women strived to be
Every impossibility.

These women proved to me,
there's so much I could achieve …

If I recognized the glory that is within me.

Dear Jen,

*I could never really tell her
How much she's meant to me.
I could never freeze the hourglass
Bring back her security.*

*For, I could never be her mother.
Keep her sheltered from the world.
I could never rock her in my arms
And whisper, "My poor, little, girl."*

*I could never give her all the things
She receives from her friends.
But, when she craves a piece of home
I can be there for her, then.*

Simply Love...

You asked me *why* do I stay?
and I said that "I love you."
You then asked to tell you *why* that is?
and I responded, I simply do.

You seemed so disheartened by my reply,
and I now know why that was...
There's more that keeps the two of us grounded.
So much more than ... simply love.

There's the long glance that you give me
when I'm rushing quickly by.
That says, "I love that woman
and I'm so damn glad she's mine."

There's the gentle way you touch me
handling with so much care.
Making sure that I feel pleasure
as your love for me is declared.

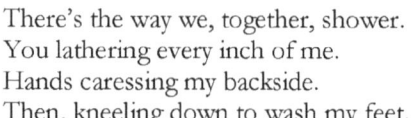

There's the way we, together, shower.
You lathering every inch of me.
Hands caressing my backside.
Then, kneeling down to wash my feet.

There's the invitation to join you
as the water fiercely steams,
much too hot for your own liking
but you know it's just right for me.

There's the way you tightly grasped my hand
at the delivery of our children.
...to be anywhere else on this earth
would have never even been an option.

There's the way you sit & play with them
and recognize how they're unique.
There's the way you'll get them dressed for church
and not just leave that job to me.

There's the way you pick up around the house
when every day is through.
The way you "lock up" and make me feel safe
to be right here with you.

There's the way that you find beauty
in every stretch mark on my tummy.
And the way you compliment me
when I feel I'm looking crummy.

I'm not trying to make it all sound splendid
I know we argue and neglect.
We have both been deeply saddened,
but no love is ever perfect.

You asked why I was drawn to you?
Why it was with you I chose to go?
You said there wasn't much to you.
But sweetie, there was much more than you know.

You were faithful from the very start.
Your fidelity was never in question.
Making me feel (everyday) that (to you)
there's no more beautiful a woman.

You listened to me, introduced me to things
I'd probably never try.
You promised (and delivered) a *beautiful* home
and with **your** love, you brightened my life.

Here and Now, Love Always.

Love in its many forms
Is...everything and anything
Ever dreamt, desired,
Feared and able and unable
To be imagined.

There are *many, many* ways...to love.

Love in its simplest...*purest* form
Is felt...without consciousness,
Without effort,
Without conscience.

It is with pain.
It is without limits
(transcending time, distance,
barriers and reason).

Pure Love may be replaced
(by *practical* love)
yet,
Pure, Primal, Passionate Love
seeps into the sinews beneath the skin,
marks its memory
and never, ever fades.

I love that I have loved...
                                    purely.

Legends
-J

Ballads,
　　　Sonnets,
　　　Novellas

Fairytales,
　　　Poetic
　　　Narratives.

Rethinking
Re-experiencing
Re-envisioning

　　　The events of our lives.

Telling of stories held
　　　In safety
　　　In fear
　　　In memoriam

Of times... Before

Telling of stories released
In safety
In faith
In honor of

A new legend.

Allowing completion
Of thoughts that linger.

(Once historic missions completed
Are purged
It makes s p a c e

for fresh stories to unfold).

Destiny brings together
Story Tellers

Him and Her

Past and Present

Models for the Future

Learning from Previous Sagas
While
Creating
an entirely revolutionary ...

EVER AFTER.

You and I are "Living" stories.

We. Are. Legends.

Conclusions
Conclusions

I Get IT: *The Cord that is WE*

I awake.
I cry.
I take.
a breath
and then, I need.

I need sleep.
I am weak.
I need.
I NEED!
And then, I breathe.

I am new.
I delight.
I'm cute.
I am love. I am *you*.

I object.
I never seem to rest.
I test
the waters making waves.

I love.
I hate.
I unwaveringly debate.
I learn to negotiate.

I know all.
"I'm right!"
I never call.
I am beauty, full.

I am lost.
I fall short.
I fear, I weep,
I plead.

When You reveal to me
what it is You need from me,
I will Be. See. Retrieve.
Breathe
it into being.

For all that I achieve.
For the glory that You receive.
It is through these
that I
find peace.

Hindsight

Next time, I will be careful.
Next time, I'll take it slow.
Next time, I'll have a guard posted
by that gate. He should not go.

Next time, I will wear protection.
Next time, I will wear a frown.
Next time, I will have a guard posted
… a guard who won't back down.

Next time, I will keep my composure.
Next time, I will feel nothing when rubbed.
Next time, I'll have a guard posted
… one who has never been in love.

Visions

I do not know
what sensations
others
experience
when they see
or talk
to

the
"*new*"
me.

I am not convinced
of what
the "new" me sees,
when she is
trapped
in a memory
of

the
"old"
me.

Yet, I do often wonder

who I will find

when I

strip down

from

this person's walk
and
that person's talk,

that woman's eyes,
and
this woman's hair,

and

Give Up

on
attempting
to
transform
into
the person

that

no one
would have
ever

expected

me

to be.

What do **I** want
and
What do **I** need?

How would **I** walk
and
how would **I** talk?

What is it
in me
that
I try
so relentlessly
to mask,
with
the
facade
of the
only
person

you

seem
able

to

love?

What Dreams?

What dreams will I make come true?

I was often told, "It's all up to you."
"There's nothing in this world that you can't do.
*But, never for one moment think you won't have **the most** to prove."*

It was preached that every situation could be improved
if I stood on my own and became no man's fool.

I was never taught how to choose a good man
or told to stick by him and love as hard as I can.

I needed nothing more than a dream
and a plan.

What dreams will I make come true?

I used to dream of taking care of you.
Until the day when one became two.
Then, I dreamt of all I still had to do.

I began to dream of being rescued:
being a partner in a love that grew,
being able to trust and commit,
saying, "I do" – and never second guessing it.

What dreams will I make come true?

I dreamt of a family, a home and some pets,
a meaningful job and remaining physically fit.
I'd skillfully balance the whole act
and never allow myself to look back.

I'd raise children in God's light.
I'd set an example, be the perfect wife.
I'd pledge to be worthy of such gifts.
I'd vow to give all I had to give.

What dreams will I make come true...?

...the dream that's unfulfilled without you?
...the dream I've tried not to see?
...the dream maybe never meant to be?

...the dream I dreamt once upon a time?
...the dream that has never left my mind?

...the dream that caused us so much pain?
...the dream that makes me so ashamed?

What dreams will I make come true?

I've so many but am a part of others' too.
*I cannot make them **all** come true:*
My dreams, your dreams, and their dreams, too.

So, what dreams will I make come true?

...the one that says, I am so in love with you?

...the one that says, there will always be two?

or

...the one that forces me to choose?

Holding TYE

Empty your mind, your heart and your soul.

Pour out any need you might possess

release any expectation you may hold

sit with the levity of being gutted,

a dry vessel,

spacious container,

an open receptacle.

What will you grant permission to enter you today?

There are no fees, requirements or rewards.

How much are you willing to absorb?

This is your commitment…today.

Contain *this*.

Protect *this*.

Today.

Now, empty your mind…

The Hope

"Baby, you will learn
that your trust must be earned."

"Girl, time and youth rush too quickly by -
respect thy temple. Hold your crown high."

"Woman, you are the Empress of a Kingdom,
the President of a Nation,

all that's feared to crumble in your presence
can be reborn with your imagination."

Who am I?

My stomach's still flabby
    and I sit with a slouch.
My frame is quite small,
    but my behind sticks way out.

My thoughts are quite deep.
    My intentions...the best.
Yet when I open my mouth
    all the words are a mess.

My nails are so brittle.
    I can't grow my hair.
For the past six years
    I've had pimples from ear to ear.

My footsteps are heavy
    I walk like a clown.
Throughout high school
    the word was that I got around.

I changed my nickname to Buddy
    for their personal amusement.
The State of Origin on my Birth Certificate
    reads State of Confusion.

I have sought out approval
    through my struggles and strife.
I guess it's ironic I've walked in
    rejection every day of my life.

Do you need more clues?
I'll give you just one.
The person I am
    has housed the person I've become.

Who I am is a person
    who has not yet been saved.
Who I've become is a person
    who prays hard for that day.

I know it will come
    with patience… in time.
For His plan is nothing
    like yours or like mine.

I have started my journey
    which does not change the facts.
But gives me insight & understanding
    when I begin to look back.

I have faith there is somewhere
    beyond space & beyond time.
Someone knows my intentions
    and is reading my mind.

He has given me ways
    of coping with stress.
I am surviving the heartache
    so I also know…I Am Blessed.

JUNE AFFIRMATIONS

I am short
I am thin
I am Powerful to the end.
I am light complexioned
and my shape is without one thing
out of place.
I can give a tender, gentle kiss
that would send shivers through your skin.

I was told it was good, quite a bit
and that my talent was in my hips.
I have been held many times
by young men who were DAMN FINE.

I can't remember every name
   every Lester
     every Dave.
I can't remember every touch
   every quiver
     every rub.
I can't remember every scene
   whether in my house
    their house
      the Jeep?

I can't remember all of it
  for I overcame
    my selflessness.

I am still short
I am still thin
I am still powerful to the end.
I am light complexioned
and my shape, is still without
one thing
out of place.

But now, I am 100x's
　　　　the woman I was
I am the lover of a new man,
　　　　his name is God.
He's given me love and trust and faith.
He's taken my pain and shame away.

I am now a college student on the Dean's List.
I am a writer,
　　　　an athlete,
　　　　an artist.
I am still loved,
　　　　but now it comes
　　　　from the most important male in my life,
　　　　　　　　my son.
I can still give you those things
　　　　you can't live without
Above all, a woman
　　　　of whom you can be proud.

I can not remember where I entered your lives
　　　　before I realized I was blessed;
Still, I will never forget
　　　　where I left.

I Discover

As He talks
And I ...pause

I Discover

As the ebony ends
And shiny silver blends

I Discover

As they age
And birth babes

I Discover

As trust is betrayed
And air thickens day by day

I Discover

As busied tones
who've watched me grow
stretch miles & miles
to keep *me* composed

I Discover

As perfection
Escapes grasp
As I trip forward
And fall back

As the picture
fades to black
And it is clear
what it lacks

I Discover

As one mourns
over a grave
the day another rejoices
in His Saving Grace

I Discover

When a child
Calls out my name
When they plot the rules
To a newly formed game

When they stammer
When they stop
When they giggle
When they hop
When they question
When they disobey
When they bargain
When they 'behave'
When they tell stories
Without end
When it appears it's over
And they add, "... an(d)...d*(th)*en……….."

I Discover

I Discover
As He reaches
In my mind
And uncovers things
I could not find
As He touches my soul
As He helps me search for gold

I Discover

I Discover
That what I want
May not be mine
And what I already possess
Is one of a kind

I Discover
That this may or may not
Be the end of the line
But that the Lord
Makes everything fine:

In ***His*** time

As I've Discovered.

The Man Who Raised Me

He's so quiet in the role He played;
    the Man who raised me.
He's so gentle with the love He gave;
    the Man who tamed me.
He's so quickly ready to embrace;
    The Man who saved me.
He, with His mystical ever-loving grace;
    He, who forgave me.

Wading

In wading,
I've been searching for
that which is pure...is truth

In waiting,
I've been hoping
that I would find my youth.

...that trust would come so easy.
...that smiles made home my face.
...that seasons had distinctions.
...that I'd a lineage I could trace.

though pained – could not be broken
each love would renew my heart.
For with each loved one's whisper
new promises, fresh starts.

Moments would dwell forever.
...reliving memories without fade.
Aging with anticipation
of many more *joyous days.*

Indestructible my desires...
Destiny appearing clear...
On the threshold of my imagined future
I could conquer anything I dared.

The still and quiet waters...
The young girl who plays ashore
pauses
jus' long enough to catch a glimpse of me
and wonder what I'm waiting for.

Gifted

With all things rare, there comes a certain divinity.

A golden image of what's been won.
A bright prediction of who's to come.

Amidst the cheers and tears of joy.
There lives a weary, sullen void.

Someone, in silence, pays its cost.
With no one else knowing, all that's been lost.

INVENTION

Every flow
is one we've known

Every Re, Do, Me
has only a hint of originality

Every verse
has once been spoken

Every song
has once been sung

Every testimony witnessed
has a parent & will birth a son

Every novice story told
that causes tears of sympathy to bloom

Strokes a nerve of the familiar
As we recall humming the very *same* tune.

JOURNEYS
- Conclusion

Journey.

What a beautiful name of mystical intent.

The Journeys I take inside,
Inside my head,
Lead me to a world of Perfect Understanding.

The view from behind
the tunnels of my eyes,
Is too tempting not to follow.

I walk alone
and though my arms
reach out into the darkness
They are not met.

Yet, I sense a presence
So strong
So overwhelmingly tender,
That it cloaks me
and holds me
Suspended.

I cease in my journey.
Turning to seek out
my companion.

Such a foolish Explorer of the Unknown;
Discoverer of wasted time, broken hearts
& E n d l e s s Doubts.

A powerful cool breeze, 360 degrees,
Turns me.
It directs me,
and sets me at a faithful pace on my so desired path.

I stand.

Fingertips frozen solid.
Hands outstretched.
Eyes sealed;
For They Can No Longer Be Trusted To Lead Me.

Slowly, my inner lids begin to reveal
A jagged image
and the reflection off a shard piece of glass
Initiates THE CYCLE.

Can I Trust?

Can I Love?

> Can I give up?
> Can I give in?

Can I Be Alone?

> Can I Be Strong?

CAN I BE WHOLE?

As it reaches completion
I open my eyes
and Face the Light.

I am reminded
of the one
whose experiences
I chronicle
and I am lost
in myself
again.

Her visits
Are often greeted
With resistance.

Her company is a mighty paradox.

When
Daring and Intrepid
Her belief in the ability
To manipulate
Her surroundings

Is a source of fortitude.

Yet, on this journey

to foster growth

When
Fearful and Lonely,
Eagerly Experimenting
With S t a b i l i z a t i o n ...

Her reoccurring dreams
Create pebbles
In my path.

She embraces me.

I am hesitant
To welcome her.

She is my unknown familiar.

Yet,
I acknowledge her
and am forever
compelled
to protect her.

As she questions…

Was not my package *always* labeled
with its Final Destination?

In a world of never-ending stories,
If You Knew You Could Not Join Me …

Why Did You Grant Yourself Permission
To Love Me?

Special Thanks ...

to You
for investing your valuable resources toward this humble offering.

*Your presence, in this moment and interest in this work, is a gift I **deeply** appreciate.*
Thank you! ❤

Journeys.[©] *is blessed in life and spirit by my Creator.*
For its start and completion is due only to This Life Source,
I refer to as, God.

In addition, I would like to honor my many aunts, uncles, & cousins,
especially those
who have provided a listening ear & loving heart,
during the times that have challenged me the most.

Also, many thanks to my amazing parents,
my beautiful sister, my precious children, nieces & nephews,
and my personal Circle of Awareness (you know who you are and my love for you).

I was once told that I come from a long line of powerful people.
All of them have touched my life in such special ways that I want to give
Love, Thanks & Praise to each and every member of my family.

To the children (and young adults) of the village,
our precious wildflowers in the valley,
Surround yourselves with unconditional love, faith and support
– you will in all ways deserve these (and so much more).

To my husband, the earth, the sun, the rain, and the stars:
You helped me to find my roots and watched me bloom.
*Rain or Shine, YOU are truly **my** angel.*

T, Tyona, Mommy, Auntie, Ty ❤

WHY?

Mom tells me
my questions
are very good!

But, that answers
don't always come
when we think they should.

"When will I find out?"
I ask
excitedly.

She responds,
"God will decide that, Honey,
not me."

She says,
keep asking my questions
& wondering, why?

But to be
very patient
when awaiting replies.

Mom says
sometimes answers
come right away

And others
God saves
for a more Perfect Day.

Mom says
we must trust God
with all our heart & know

When the time is right,
our answers,
he'll show.

 ♥ME ♥

The sculpture I see
Beautiful and free
Rounded...Complete

She is NEW to me.

Childhood taunts and exclusion
Hidden in eyes.
Yet, her view is unclouded.

She is Centered.

She is WISE.

Awkwardness of Adolescence:
'Mosquito Bumps' and acne scars,

nourished her children,

pleasured her husband,

framed her face...as she smiled.

Once she thought a made-up face
was all it took to erase
all that was done to devastate.

Now, she reveals:

Her eyes, the sleepless nights.
Her hair has lost its shine.
Her cheeks, well, they've some lines.

But she is FINE.

The model-standard
peek-a-boo-ready belly,
tight ass,
and slender thighs

The Artist has replaced
with vivacious,
eye-catching,
head-turning curves
...Over Time.

Created with sugar
and a hint of spice

Sand-filled bricks
form her hips.

Above her chin
plump & fruity,
strawberry-juicy
lips.

Carved from stone
Encased in glass

Water-flowing

Vision toting

Willing to surrender
If, kindly, asked.

But, what everyone wants,
believes and thinks
won't determine whether
she grows, maintains or shrinks.

She takes no orders,
demands, or unreasonable requests.
When she is tired
she allows herself rest.

NO REGRETS!

No. No superhuman missions
or failed quests.

There are no definitions
To define HER success.

No search for family
or feeling that
something's 'just wrong.'

What she is a part of
she treasures.
What eludes her
must not have belonged.

Not contemporary, classic,
old-school smooth,
or pop-culture's best.

Not Bohemian-modern
or Afro centric
But, a piece of art, none-the-less.

Looking at her composition
From her hair to her feet

I can't help but take a breath,
laying my fingers upon my chest,
Whispering (sincerely)

"I am so impressed by what I see."

Neither a puzzle,
nor mystery.

Complex... yet complete.

I am in love with

The NEW ♥ me

Epilogue- Landings

A
t last printing, I was nervously researching the worlds of copyright licensing, literary agents, and self-publishing. After receiving my first copyright certification for the first edition of Journeys©, I proudly but cautiously distributed the manually printed and bound book to five family members. Eventually, years later, another copy was timidly given to two others. Yes, decades of handwritten, then ink-typed, then keyboard entered, typeset, PC-edited, and categorized writings had journeyed from my heart, to diaries, to typewriter rollers, to 3.5-inch floppy disks, to Compact Disks, to memory cards, to a printer, cutting & binding machines, resting in the hands and hearts of less than a dozen people.

I had not conceptualized a plan for the widespread distribution of my feelings, and what sometimes felt like foolishness, flaws, and failures. In Journeys©, I exposed myself in *(almost)* every conceivable light. Handing over heartfelt ponderings and youthful naïveté to a small group of others dearest to me felt "brave-enough," at the time.

Drafting, *"Preface - The Window,"* provided a framed picture of protection. The illusion of safety. *I am still unsure whether my completion of this book is meant to serve as a window into my soul... maybe, it will be a window into your own.* - I am aware there exists a multiplicity of views of this presented portrait.

O
nce this passes into unknown hands, lights may dim, windows may shatter. I will instantly lose control of where the old and new pieces of me land, and the light in which each word I've released is viewed.

This is much of what still binds me.

When the first edition of Journeys was completed with its 75 carefully selected poems, I was just exiting my twenties; a daughter, a sister, a friend, a wife, mother of three young sons, a case manager, a supervisor, a clinician, and an educator.

In the next 20 years, much of the unimaginable manifested itself. I tended to & began mending many invisibly fractured relationships with men in my life, including my father. I learned to fall so deeply in gratitude for every tear, *tear* and rupture as each one revealed critical lessons.

In 2008, I resigned from my full-time position and became a daily caregiver for my mother who suffered a brain injury several years before. In the last 16 years, spending each day with my mother and paternal grandmother, I've learned so many sacred stories of their lives. Young women, mothers, and girls. Learning to survive the tensions of fear and love. Also, that year, as I came to companion my girlhood caregivers in our new roles, and complementary & contrasting walks through womanhood, *I* birthed a girl.

The birth of each of my four children has changed my life. They are extraordinary beings. After each emerged into the world, I reexamined my existence: my past life's conflictual choices. Moments of slow and speedy metamorphosis, as I waded through the overpowering waves of my own fear, purpose, passion and longing for a love that felt pure. My firstborn strengthened my determination to set and achieve lofty goals. Searching myself to find a maturer version of self. My second born tapped into my fears of mortality, softened my heart and deepened my faith as I dove into idyllic-motherhood-wife-life, and explored passive surrender. Disappearing the multiplying fear into unknown selves. My third born awakened my inner superhero. A little grit, a little rage, a little vengeance. Leading me often to extend myself, beyond myself, to protect myself. The birth of my daughter has sharpened my worldview while vividly illuminating the shadows of my inner worlds. It has sparked a deep mourning for reuniting with the cautious wisdom shedded with selves I have abandoned. It's led me to disentangle & redefine my walk with womanhood and motivates me to be so much more tenderly heroic than I was before. New ways of being courageous are continually presenting themselves to me through my relationship with her. Including publicly publishing this poetry collection.

Moving with the weight of being young, Black, and female in a world of possibilities and impossibilities is a legacy that binds all current and former little young Black girls, including my daughter, my mother, my grandmother, and myself. Persistence. Determination. Self-advocacy. Provocation. Patience. Settling. Surrender. Acceptance. Self-love. *All* former little girls may find themselves walking through a time of seeking out suitable tools for battling and balancing these. Moving from authentically spirited to a more cautiously 'measured' woman, compromising the "wild, wise, woman-warrior within" to negotiate interpersonal conflicts in virtues and values is tremendously hard looking into the eyes of my daughter. Acting as if I can't or I won't move forward because I am afraid of what others will believe is enormously difficult when I know *she* is watching my footsteps. I do continue to be unsure if releasing parts of me for *unknown* others to read is even what I fully *want* to do. No matter what occurs, how others view me, how I stumble or fall, landings have to look more graceful when I'm aware my little girl is watching me leap.

What I am sure of is I wish for my sons and daughter to better know *me* when they struggle later in life. The 'me' that ran Cub Scout Packs, held an office position with the PTO, volunteered as room mom in multiple classrooms at once, ensured the arrival of beverages & snacks for sports teams, homeschooled, chaperoned field trips, took them to and from school, band rehearsal, sports practice, and summer camp. Purchased their favorite toys, games & clothes, organized their rooms, closets & birthday celebrations, advocated for their health, education, entertainment and mental wellbeing.

I want them to remember and know that with **that** *'me,' their mother*, there was also the 'me' that was a girl, who was welcomed into this life by teenagers, raised in a world different than they knew, who saw things they were sheltered from. A girl, who loved a boy, had huge dreams, became a mother, moved far away from her preferred home (and many of her passions), experienced heartbreak, became a young woman, met a young man, loved that young man, planned a wedding, a family, a life, and moved through that life in a cycle of adoration and devotion and heartache and planning and surprises and growing and grief and gratitude, while mothering.

My children are the best and most beautiful parts of me, being reborn, reimagined, recreated, in exponentially more astounding and remarkable forms each time one of them takes a breath. They may also one day find floating within them, inherited parts of their parents' pain. As I did. As my parents did. As their parents did. As each parent before the prior one, who was once a child soaring in an unfamiliar world, probably did.

We all can find our souls seemingly trapped in currents of our own and others' fear, love, confusion. If these fleeting moments ever visit them, I want them to know that parts of us, *all,* struggle. To understand that to be wondrously beautiful, our life *must* also contain intricate complexities, and no matter how hard we try or what careful intentions we set, at precious times, we may *all* find ourselves not *being, or sometimes even knowing,* our 'best' desired selves. We all can experience intensely meaningful moments that feel emotion-driven, foolish, flawed.

I have learned to love these moments, and I release *my* moments for them, the most beautiful parts of me, my children. So that they might more compassionately receive complicated parts of themselves, learn to listen with, and appreciate these parts, and choose to gift themselves grace, *patience - and grace*, as these parts travel to find a place of rest within them.

If you are reading this and gaining new views into your own soul's flight, I wish you more gentle awareness of any pieces of yourself still gliding along a complex journey, searching for grace-filled spaces to land.

.

Wishing you peace on your journeys.

.

About the Author

2005 ❧ 2024

Tyona Y.S.M Ezeilo grew up in the northeastern United States, spending her early childhood years in New York and New Hampshire. Later, living her adolescence in Middlesex and Mercer Counties in New Jersey before moving to Palm Beach County, Florida. Tyona earned both her bachelor's and master's degrees in social work at Florida Atlantic University. Since earning her degrees, she has worked in the social work field providing individual, family and couples counseling; facilitating therapeutic groups; coaching, as well as participating in program & professional development, reflective supervision, training and education. Currently, she serves as a caregiver, an organizational & developmental consultant, group facilitator, mindfulness teacher, life coach and grief educator. She is married and the mother of four.

TYSME

With all my shattered, scattered pieces,

I am a child of Our Creator.

My scars, handpicked by my Maker.

Marks: anticipated, deliberate remnants of her-story

to provide me a testimony,

and

Him

The Glory.

Index

Index of Poems

A–Z

Poems	Page

Poems	Page

Poems	Page

Poems	Page

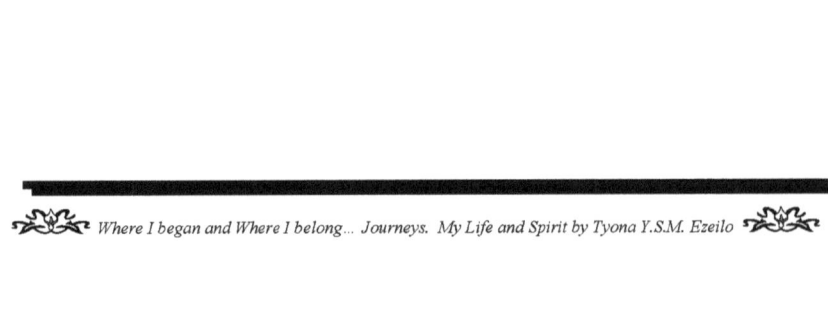

Journeys.